Raindrops

Rain Kennedy

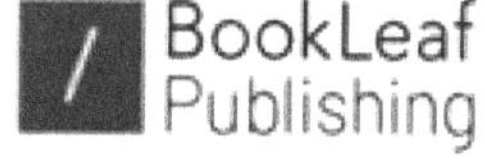

BookLeaf Publishing

Presentation by *BookLeaf Publishing*

Web: www.bookleafpub.com

E-mail: info@bookleafpub.com

ISBN : 9789357210737

First edition 2022

DEDICATION

For all of those who gave me reasons to write, thank you for pushing the words right out of me.

ACKNOWLEDGEMENT

To my tireless, unpaid, and unofficial editor, in my world full of trees, you've proven to be a hickory time and time again. Thank you for believing in me, for telling me which of my word salads suck, and which ones could make the cut. Most importantly, thank you for helping me not go crazier.

PREFACE

These are little drops and bites of my heart and soul manifested as words. Through times of extreme growth and transformation, when all was uncertain, I found safety in these words. I hope they do the same for you.

ps.

This book was proofread with a fine-toothed comb, all typos and "misspellings" have their own meaning, and are representative of their original pressing on my trusty typewriter, who sometimes has a mind of her own.

"Raindrops"

Rain drops,
Thought blots,
Drips of the sea;
  Swirling around
In this shell of me.

"Home"

looking up
        I see-
a thousand stars
or a thousand
lives?
both are mine-
lost in time,
and ready to go
        home.

"The Screaming Me's"

but what about
when the tears scream
down your face?
a stream
of soul whispers
peaking at
their not-enough
their shadows
their knowing
of your entire enveloping.

so what then?

"Dripping with Grace"

she is explosions
  of wildflowers,
an impossible sunflower field,
  where the little gold faces
  act as it
  they were clever.
  she is go big
or go home;

her focus a laser
  dialed in
the alchemy of "is"
into being flows-
a cup running over.

she is the thunderous sky,

a trailblazer of the old ways
hearing, reading and tasting
  the signs-
as if the storm were already over.

she is both
of the double rainbows,

a contradiction and ablation of colors
each one, an d angel-
a guide
as if luckier than all
of the clover.

she is the gentlest
of all fighters,

fierce in her mercy
  gracefully dripping compassion
with blood
until it is finally over.

"Breadcrumbs"

a trail
of words-
that's what
I'll leave-
breadcrumbs;
for you,
from me.

"The Whole Loaf"

I've been looking
searching for the words-
when I stopped
I found them already inside me.

"If Words were Sluts"

Sluts,

I just love
The shape of them-
All spread out
On their crisp white sheets.

I just can't resist
The lure of them-
Their coming out
Together in such raw groupings.

I just give in
To the tones-
Of their banging it out
lost in the rhythm of their impressions.

"Raindance"

She thought
Silently and violently
To herself—
This is for me,
I am the cause;

Amidst the waves of water—
This storm, she thought
Will not last,
Enjoy it while you can.
Smell of the petrichor,

Feel the energy
From the bodies
Of all the little
Raindrops, dancing
For you in this moment—

That is rare,
Breathe it in,
Let the soaking of your lungs
Be the bath
And cleansing

Of all those bodies
Dropped their life
for—
So be still,
And enjoy their sacrifice.

"And I started to chew"

And here I am,
Chewing over your words-
Though few,
They're tasty,
And give me much to ruminate.
I am seeing,
You felt as I did,
What I thought you did,
But I couldn't prove-
Your need to hide behind
The chair,
For fear of being seen-
The eyes having it,
Knowing, but not sharing
It,
The eyes never quite moving
The tongues-
You did dance
With me,
Over the rice,
I knew it-
I see that I love you
For making it safe
For me to make a mess-

To find the will
To take up space.

"Mourning Rain"

the rain,
the slow rolling train,
the me tallic ping of the air,
the drone of the fan.
the weight of your sigh,
and the hopeless heaving
        of your breathing.

"Waitsing in that Voice"

i love that sound

being the first true sound
that greets my ears,
thick and rich and scratchy-
it holds such a body and meaning
in its echoes of other worlds
still holding on to the chords
of your heart and belly sounds;
fighting, trying to come back down.
like molasses on burlap—
prickers coated in honey,
strained through a rusted metal sieve,
oozing through the stickiest
and rawest cascades
of your freshest,
and sharpest intentions;

good morning, I hear.

"Waitsing Two"

That sound,
Of oozing burlap and honey?
It is etched in my brain,
And burned in my tympanums,
Beating a buzzing inside me
Real as if it were standing
Right in front of me,
Spitting out the bites
Which I find the most delicious—
The ear worms can't help
But indulge those bits of me
Which are still chewing
Over the syllablelous luster
Left by that rusty ole sieve.

"I am the Death Card"

It seems I've ended up here,
In this place I though I was
immune—
Too close to the issue,
Lost
My overarching perspective—
I can't see the forest,
For the trees are too
close.
It seems I've lost sight
Of where all of this began
And refuse
To credit all that are due
For how much this forest has grown—
Once baby saplings littered my world—
Today
I am dwarfed by the enormity
Of this entanglement.
The warps and wefts
Are more intricate than my weaving mind
Could have visioned—
The trails winding us
Together
Though indirectly enough to make one
wonder.

Strands of light bending through
Our souls
Too close to perfection
But still searching for
Just the right photo-
Receptors so discerning in every blink—
There's still time,
But the grains are always falling—
Not thinking, just being
Exactly as we are
Meant to
be. s

"Busted"

I split it right open
Right there
On the floor
While she stared,
Unmoving, not
Knowing what to do.
"It's okay"
I said,
I'll be okay.
And the blood dripped
Into my mouth—
Brighter than the light
In the widening
of her eyes.

"I Found the Last Red Balloon"

I see a swollen balloon
Behind the walls of my belly
Still sipping in air
As full as my lungs
Right before I scream
For all that is mine.
With that balloon,
In the safety of the cushioned air,
My vortex is running,
Constantly manufacturing precursors
Of my wildest manifestations—
I see them building,
Growing, waiting
For that moment
Where it all come out
In one big whoosh,
Bursting from the whole
Of my belly button.

"Home"

It's a total ego
Trip,
The joy I get
From hearing—
If you keep doing that,
I'm going
To cu—it's cute;
They think I don't
already know,
Like it's surprise,
And not something written
All over their faces,
Etched in the lines
Of their legs,
And measured by the quickening
Of the quivers covering
Them up;
That moment,
I know unequivocally
Too well.
So well,
I recognize it now
For control masquerading
As connection.

And this,
I am ready to give up.
I want to hear—
If you keep doing that,
I'm going to
Come home.
I want to hear—

You're it.
You're the one
I've been dreaming of;
 Hoping for
Praying for,
manifesting.

You're it
 That's all.
You're the end;
you're the other half
You're it,
The welcome;
The welcome home,
The homecoming,
Come home.

"Honey, Mirror, Magic-Number Three"

The mirroring
Of all of me—
My beautiful intricacies,
Shadows, and
imperfections—
Honey,
We're both flawed.

Therein lies the depth
And madness
Of our shared
Light, and
The magic
Of the instances
Of our shared existences.

"The Case of the Disappearing Fuck"

Both of them,
They went searching
In the barely still there night—
Searching for warmth,
And the folds,
Which inherently feel right.

They set off,
With a compass uniquely pointed
Searching for an order—
Twins in many ways,
Nearly mirrored, matching; just
One a bit shorter.

Their first attempt,
Failed, ended in limp defeat
And a kind of ever elusive sleep—
Their second attempt,
Still limp; a body whispered
Promises not to keep.

They found their crevice
They found their hole,
Almost never heard from

again—
And with it
My last fuck they stole.

"The Crunchy Bits"

That first pan,
a first attempt
At something?
Long before I met
You, I was
Fat and happy.
Not really, but
I didn't know
The depths.
What I do know is that night,
I ate too much, and
I loved it.
But since I was fat
I don't really get that
Desire for more.
I always counted and watched
All that came in
Or went out.
Food was for a reason
On a good day
And a special punishment
When left unguarded.
But your fucking
paella—
I could taste the fire

Of your moon
In each bite
Of greasy, crunchy, slutty
Debauchery;
And I've had nothing better
since.

"The Last Straw"

I told you,
You started
With a whole bushel
Of straws—
Now you have
Only one,
And it's not
The one
I'm sucking on.

"Baby, it's Fucking Cold Outside"

I used to hate the cold—
The numbing bite
Of a soulless world
Waiting on the promised
Light and incurred warmth
Of the spring—
The real new year.
I would dread the tightness—
The rigidity of my skin and frame
And of my mindscape—
Reflecting the brittle bitterness
Exuding from all of everything.
I hated—and therefore blocked—
The looming darkness
The cold surely promised
The deliver at some point—
Only when most inconvenient.
But, fuck that—
I've decided to love it,
Embrace the bite
And relax into the impending
Change
Of the seasons, barometer, and
Inevitable transformation of

Mind, and then bones
As I step into this new love
For the delicate intricacies unveiled
And made prone
By the kiss of the frosty
Whispers;
Calling, crooning, drawing
Me where I've yet
To come. Regardless,
I know that when I choose
My own flavors to foster and believe,
I always love the taste
Left behind.